The Normal distribution
Unit Guide

The School Mathematics Project

b.

The right of the
University of Cambridge
to print and sell
all manner of books
was granted by
Henry VIII in 1534.
The University has printed
and published continuously
since 1584.

Cambridge University Press

Cambridge   New York   Port Chester   Melbourne   Sydney

Main authors	Chris Belsom
	Robert Black
	David Cundy
	Stan Dolan
	Chris Little
	Fiona McGill
	Mary Rouncefield
	Jane Southern

Team leader Chris Belsom

Project director Stan Dolan

Statistics programs Margaret and Peter Hayball

The authors would like to give special thanks to Ann White for her help in producing the trial edition and in preparing this book for publication.

Published by the Press Syndicate of the University of Cambridge
The Pitt Building, Trumpington Street, Cambridge CB2 1RP
40 West 20th Street, New York NY 10011–4211, USA
10 Stamford Road, Oakleigh, Victoria 3166, Australia

First published 1992

Produced by Gecko Limited, Bicester, Oxon

Cover design by Iguana Creative Design

Printed in Great Britain at the University Press, Cambridge

British Library cataloguing in publication data

A catalogue record for this book is available from the British Library.

ISBN 0 521 40881 4

Contents

Introduction to 16–19 Mathematics

Nobody reads introductions and nobody reads teachers' guides, so what chance does the introduction to this unit guide have? The least we can do is to keep it short! We hope that you will find the discussion point and tasksheet commentaries and ideas on presentation and enrichment useful.

The School Mathematics Project was founded in 1961 with the purpose of improving the teaching of mathematics in schools by the provision of new course materials. SMP authors are experienced teachers and each new venture is tested by schools in a draft version before publication. Work on *16–19 Mathematics* started in 1986 and the pilot of the course has been used by over 30 schools since 1987.

Since its inception the SMP has always offered an 'after sales service' for teachers using its materials. If you have any comments on *16–19 Mathematics*, or would like advice on its use, please write to:

16–19 Mathematics
The SMP Office
The University
Southampton SO9 5NH

Why 16–19 Mathematics?

A major problem in mathematics education is how to enable ordinary people to comprehend in a few years concepts which geniuses have taken centuries to develop. In theory, our view of how to pass on this body of knowledge effectively and pleasurably has changed considerably; but no great revolution in practice has been seen in sixth-form classrooms generally. We hope that, in this course, the change in approach to mathematics teaching embodied in GCSE schemes will be carried forward. The principles applied in the course are appropriate to this aim.

- Students are actively involved in developing mathematical ideas.
- Premature abstraction and over-reliance on algorithms are avoided.
- Wherever possible, problems arise from, or at least relate to, everyday life.
- Appropriate use is made of modern technology such as graphic calculators and microcomputers.
- Misunderstandings are confronted and acted upon.

By applying these principles and presenting material in an attractive way, A level mathematics is made more accessible to students and more meaningful to them as individuals. The *16–19 Mathematics* course is flexible enough to provide for the whole range of students who obtain at least a grade C at GCSE.

Structure of the courses

The A and AS level courses have a core-plus-options structure. Details of the full range of possibilities, including A and AS level *Further Mathematics* courses, may be obtained from the Joint Matriculation Board, Manchester M15 6EU.

For the A level course *Mathematics (Pure with Applications)*, students must study eight core units and a further two optional units. The diagram below shows how the units are related to each other. Other optional units are being developed to give students an opportunity to study aspects of mathematics which are appropriate to their personal interests and enthusiasms.

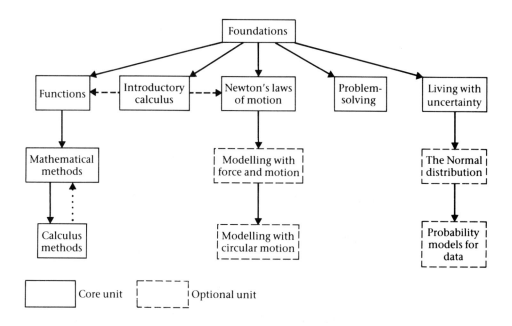

The *Foundations* unit should be started before or at the same time as any other core unit.

Any of the other units can be started at the same time as the *Foundations* unit. The second half of *Functions* requires prior coverage of *Introductory calculus*. *Newton's laws of motion* requires calculus notation which is covered in the initial chapters of *Introductory calculus*.

The Polynomial approximations chapter in *Mathematical methods* requires prior coverage of some sections of *Calculus methods*.

For the AS level *Mathematics (Pure with Applications)* course, students must study *Foundations, Introductory calculus* and *Functions*. Students must then study a further two applied units.

Material

The 16–19 Mathematics textbooks contain several devices to aid an active style of learning.

- Topics are opened up through **group discussion points**, signalled in the text by the symbol

and enclosed in rectangular frames. These consist of pertinent questions to be discussed by students, with guidance and help from the teacher. Commentaries for discussion points are included in this unit guide.

- The text is also punctuated by **thinking points**, having the shape

and again containing questions. These should be dealt with by students without the aid of the teacher. In facing up to the challenge offered by the thinking points it is intended that students will achieve a deeper insight and understanding. A solution within the text confirms or modifies the student's response to each thinking point.

- At appropriate points in the text, students are referred to **tasksheets** which are placed at the end of the relevant chapter. A tasksheet usually consists of a self-contained piece of work which is used to investigate a concept prior to any formal exposition. In many cases, it takes up an idea raised in a discussion point, examining it in more detail and preparing the way for formal treatment. There are also **extension tasksheets** (labelled by an E), for higher attaining students, which investigate a topic in more depth and **supplementary tasksheets** (labelled by an S), which are intended to help students with a relatively weak background in a particular topic. Commentaries for all the tasksheets are included in this unit guide.

The aim of the **exercises** is to check full understanding of principles and give students confidence through reinforcement of their understanding.

Graphic calculators/microcomputers are used throughout the course. In particular, much use is made of graph plotters. The use of videos and equipment for practical work is also recommended.

As well as the textbooks and unit guides, there is a **Teacher's resource file**. This file contains: review sheets which may be used for homework or tests; datasheets; technology datasheets which give help with using particular calculators or pieces of software; a programme of worksheets for more able students which would, in particular, help prepare them for the STEP examination.

Introduction to the unit (for the teacher)

This unit of the *16–19 Mathematics* course covers perhaps the most important statistical distribution. The Normal probability distribution emerges as a model for a number of continuous variables and the unit explores its central role in the study of statistics. The development is intended to provide a sound conceptual understanding of the essential ideas which are placed in practical contexts wherever appropriate.

Sufficient data sets are provided for the work, but you may choose to use other data, perhaps collected by the class. As part of the assessment, students are required to undertake a single piece of coursework. The exact nature of this will depend on the individual but a data collection which could ultimately be used to make population inferences would be appropriate. By the end of the unit students should be able to estimate confidence intervals for both mean values and proportions.

The unit is supported by a number of short computer simulations. Students are also expected to use either standard computer software or graph plotting calculators when seeking a mathematical function to describe the bell-shaped distribution. No special pure mathematical techniques are required for the study of this unit other than a familiarity with the ideas of numerical integration for finding areas under curves.

Familiarity with the exponential function would be useful but is not essential.

Chapter 1

Students initially work on a number of data sets and see the bell-shaped distribution emerge from various sets of data. To counteract the possible misconception that all data sets of this sort have bell-shaped distributions a set of data with a distinctly non-Normal distribution is also considered.

The concept of relative frequency density is introduced together with that of the relative frequency histogram. The association of the area under the distribution with probability is made.

Prior experience of curve sketching is exploited as students attempt to discover an appropriate mathematical description of the distribution. Students are also shown how to standardise data and the relevance of this idea in comparing data sets.

Chapter 2

In this chapter the Normal probability model is applied in a number of situations and the use of tables of the standard Normal function is dealt with. Various Normal distributions are employed and are reduced to the standard Normal distribution by standardising the data.

Chapter 3

In this chapter the relationship between the Normal and binomial distributions is explored. The conditions necessary to use the Normal as an approximate model for a binomial random variable are carefully considered. Formulas for the mean and variance of the binomial probability distribution are discovered with the aid of computer simulation.

Chapter 4

From this point in the text the unit explores the role of the Normal distribution in the theory of sampling. In this chapter, obtaining information about a population from a sample and the concept of sampling distributions are developed in the context of the sampling distribution of the mean. The Central Limit Theorem and its implications are discussed, as are the ideas of biased and unbiased estimators.

Chapter 5

The theme of this chapter is confidence intervals. The general idea is explored prior to its use in estimating confidence intervals for the mean based on evidence obtained from a sample. For the mean, a clear distinction is made between the case where the population variance is known and the more realistic case where the variance has to be estimated from the sample.

Chapter 6

This chapter covers the important application of estimating a confidence interval for a proportion. Use is made of earlier work on the Normal approximation to the binomial to develop appropriate formulas for the interval. Use is made of the context of opinion polls and it should be easy to provide stimulating and relevant up-to-date examples from the local or national press.

Tasksheets and resources

This list gives an overview of where tasksheets are to be used. Items in *italics* refer to resources not included in the main text.

1 An important distribution

1.1 Introduction

> Suppose you were asked to sample the heights of 100 adult males and draw a histogram. Jot down the rough shape of the histogram you would expect.
>
> Why would you expect to get the shape you have drawn?

From a sample of 100 adult males you would expect a histogram shaped like the one below.

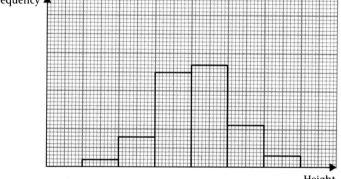

There are few men who are **very** tall or **very** short. Most men are somewhere in the middle.

1.2 A pattern emerges!

> Comment on the shapes of the various distributions considered in the tasksheet, describing their similarities and differences.
>
> Which distributions have the same shape as that for the weights of coins?

1

The distributions are similar in shape, the only exception being data set E. Data sets A, B, C and D have similar proportions of values within ± 1 s.d., ± 2 s.d., ± 3 s.d. of the mean. When compared with the distribution of the weights of coins you should find that A, B, C and D are remarkably similar and only set E is the odd one out.

1.6 Finding the function

Plot the graphs of functions of the form

$$f(x) = ke^{-\frac{1}{2}x^2}$$

and show that functions of this form have the same basic **shape** as the Normal curve. Consider different values of k, including negative values.

What other important **area** property should the function possess? How does this help in finding the required value of k?

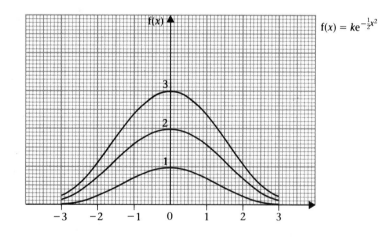

$$f(x) = ke^{-\frac{1}{2}x^2}$$

Graphs of the functions $e^{-\frac{1}{2}x^2}$, $2e^{-\frac{1}{2}x^2}$, and $3e^{-\frac{1}{2}x^2}$ are shown and clearly display the basic shape that is required.

If k is negative, then the graphs obtained are mirror images of those shown with a positive value for k. Therefore k must be positive.

The area under the curve should be 1. This idea can be used to find k by plotting $f(x)$ for different values of k and obtaining the total area under each curve using, say, the trapezium rule. You can keep adjusting k until the area is (approximately) 1.

Coins

1

Weight in grams	Tally	Frequency
6.80 –	I	1
6.85 –	I	1
6.90 –		0
6.95 –	IIII	5
7.00 –	IIII IIII	10
7.05 –	IIII IIII IIII IIII	19
7.10 –	IIII IIII IIII IIII	19
7.15 –	IIII IIII IIII IIII IIII	24
7.20 –	IIII IIII I	11
7.25 –	IIII	4
7.30 –	IIII	4
7.35 –		0
7.40 –	II	2
	Total	100

2

3 –

4 (a) ± 1 s.d. covers approximately the range of values 7.0 to 7.2. There are 72 observations (or about 70% of the observations) within ± 1 s.d. of the mean.

(b) You are looking for values below 6.9 and above 7.3 (approximately). There are 8 observations (or 8% of the observations) more than 2 s.d. from the mean.

Different variables

1   **Data set A**

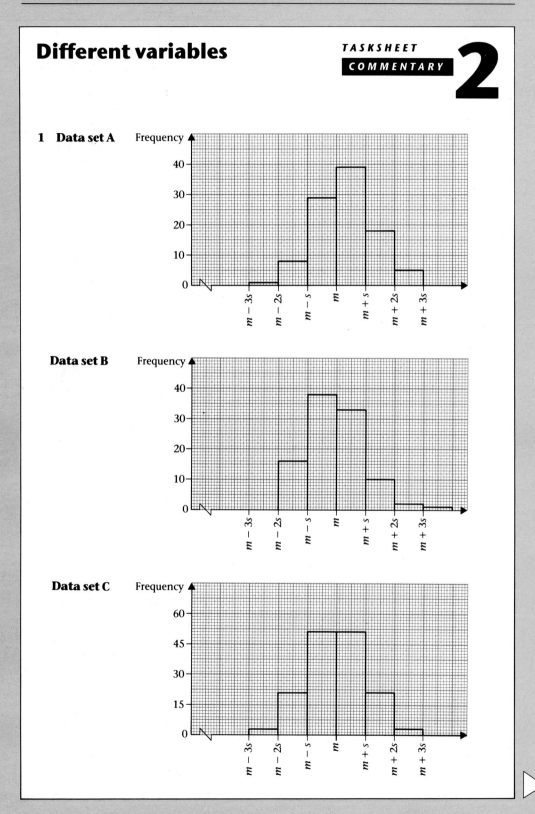

Data set B

Data set C

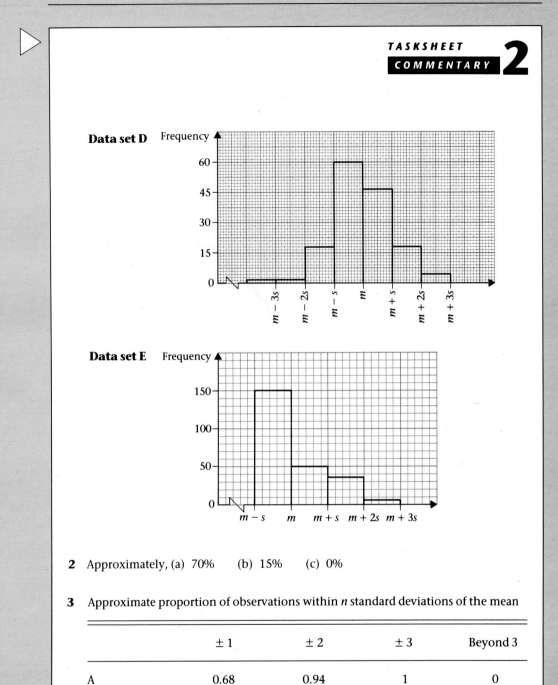

Data set D Frequency

Data set E Frequency

2 Approximately, (a) 70%   (b) 15%   (c) 0%

3 Approximate proportion of observations within *n* standard deviations of the mean

	± 1	± 2	± 3	Beyond 3
A	0.68	0.94	1	0
B	0.71	0.97	0.99	0.01
C	0.68	0.96	1	0
D	0.71	0.96	0.99	0.01
E	0.80	0.92	0.98	0.02

Area under the Normal curve

1 (a) The area under $f(x) = e^{-\frac{1}{2}x^2}$ is approximately 2.5 (to 2 s.f.).

   (b) The proportion of the area under the curve between

    (i) 0 and 1 is about 0.34 (34%)

    (ii) 1 and 2 is about 0.14 (14%)

    (iii) 2 and 3 is about 0.02 (2%)

   (c) The proportion between

    (i) 0 and $-1 = 0.34$

    (ii) -1 and $-2 = 0.14$

    (iii) -2 and $-3 = 0.02$

2 The proportions are very similar to those for each data set A–D. The differences are partly due to approximations in obtaining the area and, more importantly, because the data sets are samples of only 100 values.

3 Values of k around 0.4 give an area of approximately 1.

3 From Binomial to Normal

3.1 Binomial to Normal

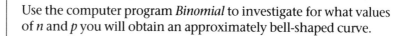

> Use the computer program *Binomial* to investigate for what values
> of n and p you will obtain an approximately bell-shaped curve.

The computer will draw the distribution B(n, p) when you provide n
and p. It is a good idea to investigate what happens for large n first
(for example $n = 200$) and to vary p.

For values of p approximately equal to 0.5 the distribution is approximately
symmetrical and bell-shaped. For large (near 1) or small (near 0) values of p
you can still obtain the bell shape by increasing n.

3.2 Using the Normal to approximate binomial distributions

> (a) A box contains 60 dice. A prize of a car is offered to anyone
> who obtains 30 or more sixes on turning out the dice from
> the box. Is it worth paying 10p for a turn?
>
> (b) Would it be worth paying 10p if the prize were £10 for 20
> or more sixes?

(a) For $X \sim$ B($60, \frac{1}{6}$) the probability of winning the car is

$$P(X = 30) + P(X = 31) + \ldots + P(X = 60)$$

$P(X = 30) = \binom{60}{30}\left(\frac{1}{6}\right)^{30}\left(\frac{5}{6}\right)^{30} \approx 2 \times 10^{-9}$. The other probabilities
are even less likely and the total probability of winning the car is
actually less than 10^{-8}.

Winning once in 10^8 turns would cost you $10^8 \times$ 10p or
£10 million. It would be much better to buy a car!

(b) Obtaining 20 or more sixes is slightly more likely.

$$P(X = 20, 21, 22, \ldots, 60) = \binom{60}{20}\left(\frac{1}{6}\right)^{20}\left(\frac{5}{6}\right)^{40} + \binom{60}{21}\left(\frac{1}{6}\right)^{21}\left(\frac{5}{6}\right)^{39} + \ldots$$
$$\approx 0.001$$

Winning £10 once in every 1000 goes would cost you £100 so,
again, it does not seem worth having a turn.

The mean and variance of the binomial distribution

1

n	p	Mean	Variance
10	$\frac{1}{2}$	5	2.5
20	$\frac{1}{2}$	10	5
20	$\frac{1}{4}$	5	3.75
40	$\frac{1}{2}$	20	10
40	$\frac{1}{4}$	10	7.5
100	$\frac{1}{2}$	50	25

2   Mean $= n \times p$

3   Variance $= np(1 - p)$
        or npq where $q = 1 - p$

4 Sampling distribution of the mean

1 Your own solution will differ from this example, which is provided as an illustration.

Sample mean weight (g)	Tally	Frequency
6.80 –		0
6.85 –		0
6.90 –	II	2
6.95 –		0
7.00 –	III	3
7.05 –	IIII IIII II	12
7.10 –	IIII IIII III	13
7.15 –	IIII IIII IIII I	16
7.20 –	II	2
7.25 –	II	2
7.30 –		0
7.35 –		0
7.40 –		0

For the parent population: mean = 7.13
variance = 0.010

For the sample of size 2 given above: mean (of 50 samples) = 7.13

2 The frequency distribution of the sample means is shown below.

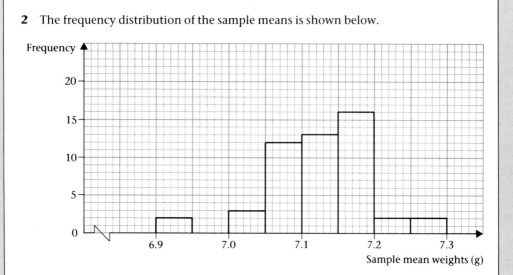

3 The mean of the distribution is 7.13.

The variance of the distribution is 0.0049.

4 The mean of the distribution of the sample means is very close to the population mean, but the variance of the sample means is smaller than the population variance. It is known that the parent population is Normally distributed.

The histogram suggests that the distribution of the sample means is also approximately Normal.

Coins 2

1 In each case, a sample of 4 is selected from the population and the mean of the sample is recorded. The histogram showing the results will be approximately bell-shaped (Normal). The mean value, which will, of course, depend on your own computer run, will be approximately equal to the population mean.

2 The distribution remains approximately bell-shaped but it becomes tighter – its variance decreases as n increases.

3 –

4 Your graph of variance against n should be of the form:

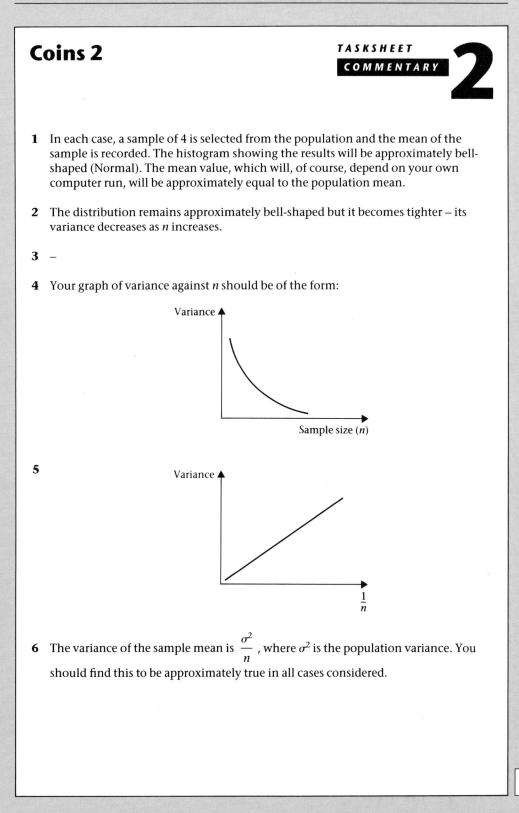

5

6 The variance of the sample mean is $\dfrac{\sigma^2}{n}$, where σ^2 is the population variance. You should find this to be approximately true in all cases considered.

Non-Normal distributions

The mean of the distribution of sample means should be close to the population mean and again the variance should be given by $\dfrac{\sigma^2}{n}$.

1 The parent population is certainly not symmetric. The distribution of sample means is not bell-shaped in the case where n is small ($n = 2$) but becomes more obviously bell-shaped as n increases.

2 (a) The mean of the sampling distribution is always approximately equal to the population mean.

   (b) Similarly, the variance is $\dfrac{\sigma^2}{n}$ in each case.

3 The distribution of the sample means always has variance $\dfrac{\sigma^2}{n}$.

5 Estimating with confidence

5.1 How clean is our water?

> (a) What justification is there for using the mean pH of a sample as an estimate for the mean pH of Clean Valley's water supply?
>
> (b) Assuming that the scientific method of each group was of the same standard, do you think the water of Clean Valley is safe to drink? Whose evidence would you take most seriously? Discuss your reasons.

(a) In chapter 4 you saw that the distribution of sample means has the same mean as the population. So, if class 5 continued taking samples of 25 jars of water, you would expect all their various values for the pH to average out at the actual mean pH of the river. The single value they obtained is therefore called an **unbiased estimator** of the population mean. You have also seen that the larger the sample size, the more tightly clustered is the distribution of possible sample means. An estimate based upon a sample mean is therefore more reliable when the sample size is large.

(b) The mean pH values for the water from Clean Valley, as calculated by two of the groups, fall within EEC guidelines, although the value obtained by the environmental group lies outside the recommended range. This value was based on a smaller sample (5 samples) and is therefore less reliable.

Care must be taken when considering results obtained by groups which have particular interests. In this instance, a large sample obtained by an independent group would be necessary.

5.3 Confidence intervals

> What proportion of sample means are within 2 standard errors of the true population mean? Calculate another confidence interval which you are much more confident contains the true population mean.

Approximately 95% of sample means fall within two standard errors of the population mean. The figure taken from the Normal tables is in fact 95.4%. To be more confident of providing an interval estimate that contains the true population mean, you would simply quote a wider confidence interval.

5.5 Estimating a population variance

> Explain the entries in the table above.
>
> Calculate a similar table for samples of size 3.
>
> For both $n = 2$ and $n = 3$, explain how your results illustrate the fact that $\bar{x}$ is an unbiased estimator of μ.

Sample	$(-1, -1, -1)$	$(-1, -1, 1)$	$(-1, 1, 1)$	$(1, 1, 1)$
Probability	$\frac{1}{8}$	$\frac{3}{8}$	$\frac{3}{8}$	$\frac{1}{8}$
Sample mean, $\bar{x}$	-1	$-\frac{1}{3}$	$\frac{1}{3}$	1
Sample variance	0	$\frac{8}{9}$	$\frac{8}{9}$	0

For both $n = 2$ and $n = 3$, the distributions of sample means have mean 0, illustrating the fact that $\bar{x}$ is an unbiased estimator of μ.

5.6 Populations with unknown variance

> (a) From these data, can you calculate the standard error of the mean remission time?
>
> (b) Do you know the population standard deviation in this case? What could you use instead?
>
> (c) Do you think the distribution of remission time is likely to be Normal? Is the distribution of **mean** remission time Normal?

(a) To find the standard error you must know the population standard deviation.

(b) You do not know the value of the population standard deviation. You have seen that $\dfrac{ns^2}{n - 1}$ is an unbiased estimator of the population variance and this could be used instead of the unknown value.

(c) If a sample is large enough then the distribution of mean remission times will be Normal, whatever the distribution of the parent population.

Confidence intervals

(a) Any particular confidence interval either contains μ or it does not.

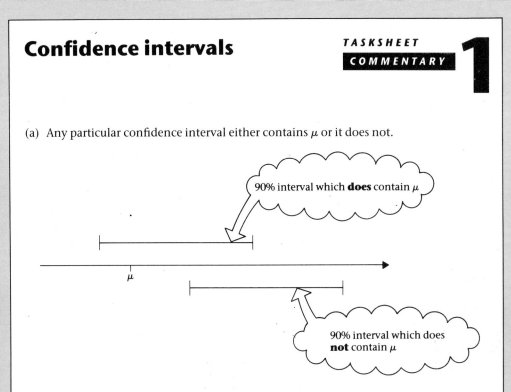

90% interval which **does** contain μ

90% interval which does **not** contain μ

You will see 5 such intervals as you run the computer program and 1000 such intervals are actually calculated. When you use an appropriate value of k, approximately 90% of your intervals will contain the true mean μ.

You should obtain a value of k which is somewhere in the range 1.6 to 1.7.

Your 90% confidence interval for μ from a particular sample of size n, mean $\bar{x}$, will be

$$\bar{x} - k\frac{\sigma}{\sqrt{n}} < \mu < \bar{x} + k\frac{\sigma}{\sqrt{n}}$$

You should confirm that your value of k allows you to find a 90% confidence interval when you estimate the mean for different Normal distributions. (Input different values of μ and σ.)

(b) You should find that approximately 95% of your intervals will contain the true population mean when $k = 1.96$.

15

Boxes of matches

1 $\mu = 47(0.2) + 48(0.6) + 49(0.2)$
$\quad = 48$

$\sigma^2 = 0.4$

2 $\bar{x} = 48.5$ when one box contains 48 matches and the other box contains 49 matches. The probability of box 1 having 48 and box 2 having 49 is 0.12, as is the probability of box 1 having 49 and box 2 having 48.
Thus the probability that $\bar{x}$ is $48.5 = 2 \times 0.12 = 0.24$

3 (a) The mean value of the distribution of $\bar{x}$ is
$$47 \times 0.04 + 47.5 \times 0.24 + 48 \times 0.44 + 48.5 \times 0.24 + 49 \times 0.04 = 48$$

   (b) The mean value of the distribution of s^2 is
$$0 \times 0.44 + 0.25 \times 0.48 + 1 \times 0.08 = 0.2$$

4 For a **rectangular** population, $\mu = 48 \quad \sigma^2 = \frac{2}{3}$.

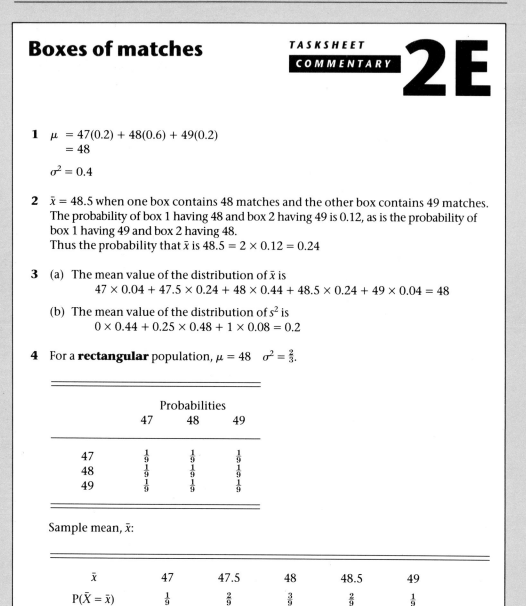

	Probabilities		
	47	48	49
47	$\frac{1}{9}$	$\frac{1}{9}$	$\frac{1}{9}$
48	$\frac{1}{9}$	$\frac{1}{9}$	$\frac{1}{9}$
49	$\frac{1}{9}$	$\frac{1}{9}$	$\frac{1}{9}$

Sample mean, $\bar{x}$:

$\bar{x}$	47	47.5	48	48.5	49
$P(\bar{X} = \bar{x})$	$\frac{1}{9}$	$\frac{2}{9}$	$\frac{3}{9}$	$\frac{2}{9}$	$\frac{1}{9}$

The mean value of the distribution of $\bar{x}$ is 48.

Sample variance, s^2:

y	0	0.25	1
P(s^2 is y)	$\frac{3}{9}$	$\frac{4}{9}$	$\frac{2}{9}$

The mean value of the distribution of s^2 is $\frac{1}{3}$.

For an **asymmetrical** population, $\mu = 47.5$ $\sigma^2 = 0.45$

	Probabilities		
	47	48	49
47	0.36	0.18	0.06
48	0.18	0.09	0.03
49	0.06	0.03	0.01

Sample mean, $\bar{x}$:

$\bar{x}$	47	47.5	48	48.5	49
P($\bar{X} = x$)	0.36	0.36	0.21	0.06	0.01

The mean value of the distribution of $\bar{x}$ is 47.5.

Sample variance, s^2:

y	0	0.25	1
P($s^2 = y$)	0.46	0.42	0.12

The mean value of the distribution of s^2 is 0.225.

For a **u-shaped** population, $\mu = 48$ $\sigma^2 = 1$.

	Probabilities		
	47	48	49
47	0.25	0	0.25
48	0	0	0
49	0.25	0	0.25

Sample mean, $\bar{x}$:

$\bar{x}$	47	47.5	48	48.5	49
$P(\bar{X} = \bar{x})$	0.25	0	0.5	0	0.25

The mean value of the distribution of $\bar{x}$ is 48.

Sample variance, s^2:

y	0	0.25	1
$P(s^2 = y)$	0.5	0	0.5

The mean value of the distribution of s^2 is 0.5.

In all of these populations you will have found that:

- the mean value of the distribution of $\bar{x}$ is μ;
- the mean value of the distribution of s^2 is $\frac{1}{2}\sigma^2$.

Another distribution

The simulation should confirm that even in this case, with a rectangular distribution, $k = 1.96$ and $k = 1.64$ provide the required confidence intervals for the population mean ($\mu = 5$).

Although the rectangular distribution is, of course, not Normal, it is symmetrical and is like the Normal distribution in this respect. If the distribution were not symmetrical then you **could** still obtain satisfactory confidence intervals but you would need **bigger** samples.

The distribution of sample means for samples taken from the rectangular distribution will still be Normally distributed for relatively small sample sizes.

Population — Mean μ — Variance σ^2 — x

Sampling distribution of the mean ($\bar{x}$) — Mean μ — Variance $\dfrac{\sigma^2}{n}$ — $\bar{x}$

This result is, of course, what you would expect from the predictions of the Central Limit Theorem.

You should note also the relative widths of the 95% and 90% confidence intervals. For a fixed sample size n ($n = 25$ here) the only way to be more confident (95% rather than 90%) is to widen the interval.

6 Population proportions

6.1 How many are there?

> If 5 of the 40 fish caught are marked, what should be her estimate of the total number of fish in the lake?
>
> How accurate do you think this estimate will be?

If you assume that the marked fish have mixed freely with others in the lake and that the recapture of 40 fish is a random sample of fish in the lake, then the proportion of marked fish in the catch is an estimate of the proportion of marked fish in the lake:

i.e.

$$\frac{5}{40} = \frac{50}{N} \text{ where } N \text{ is the number of fish in the lake}$$

The estimate of N (based on this information) is 400.

It is likely that the estimates would vary considerably from sample to sample and it is likely that repeated sampling would be necessary to improve confidence in any estimate of the population. In reality, of course, this may not be possible.

It would be interesting if you could discuss how such problems are actually dealt with, perhaps by using examples from biology or geography. You might find out, for example, how population sizes of rare species such as whales are obtained.

Sampling fish

The number of coloured tiles in your sample of 25 will, of course, vary from sample to sample. If there are x coloured tiles in your sample, then the only estimate you can make for the proportion of coloured tiles in the bag is $\dfrac{x}{25}$.

If n coloured tiles were placed in the bag so that there were N tiles altogether then

$\dfrac{x}{25}$ is your estimate of $\dfrac{n}{N}$

and your estimate of the number of tiles N in the bag will be:

$$N = \frac{25n}{x}$$

The mean value of your estimates uses more information and would provide a better estimate.

> How good a method do you think this is?
>
> Give a reason for your answer.

You will have noticed considerable variation in the estimates, so you can have little confidence in any particular estimate.

If the estimator you are using for the number of tiles in the bag is to be unbiased then its mean value should equal the population value it is estimating. The estimator, $\dfrac{25n}{x}$, is not defined when $x = 0$ (when you 'catch' no coloured tiles) and so it is not possible to obtain a mean value. The estimate N is biased.

Opinion polls

1 (a) $p = 0.348$ $q = 0.652$ $n = 9502$

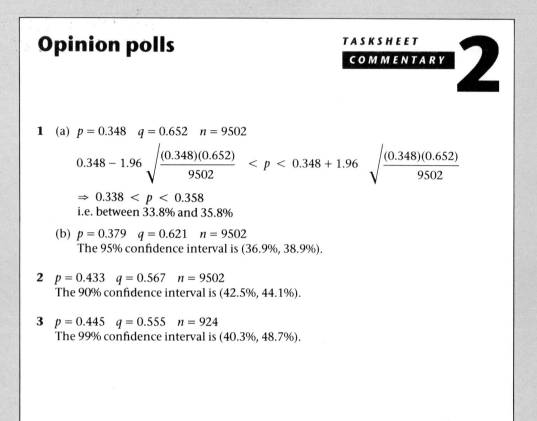

$$0.348 - 1.96\sqrt{\frac{(0.348)(0.652)}{9502}} < p < 0.348 + 1.96\sqrt{\frac{(0.348)(0.652)}{9502}}$$

$\Rightarrow 0.338 < p < 0.358$
i.e. between 33.8% and 35.8%

   (b) $p = 0.379$ $q = 0.621$ $n = 9502$
The 95% confidence interval is (36.9%, 38.9%).

2 $p = 0.433$ $q = 0.567$ $n = 9502$
The 90% confidence interval is (42.5%, 44.1%).

3 $p = 0.445$ $q = 0.555$ $n = 924$
The 99% confidence interval is (40.3%, 48.7%).